SLOTH
COLORING BOOK

Join our mailing list to be among
the first to find out about special offers,
discounts and our new releases!

Sign up at:
www.adultcoloringworld.net

ISBN-13: 978-1542393171
ISBN-10: 1542393175

PREVIEW IMAGES

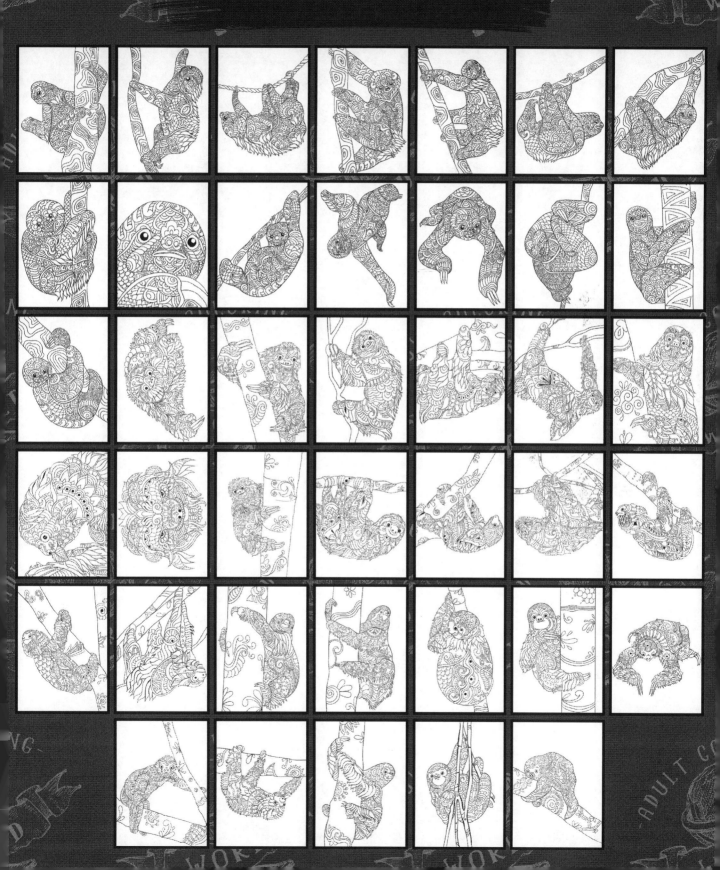

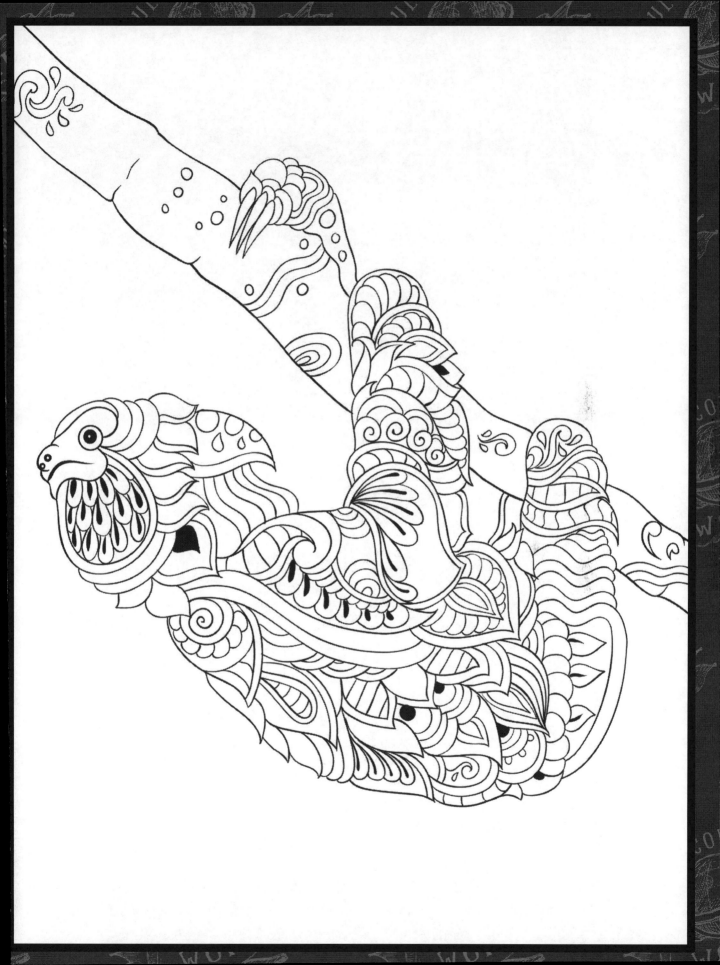

COLOR TEST
PAGE

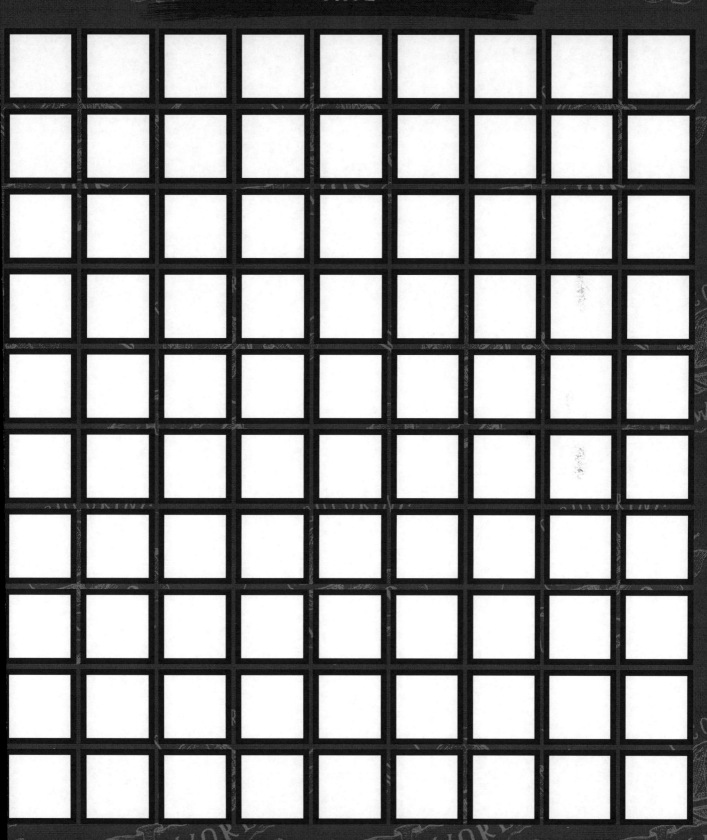

COLOR TEST
PAGE

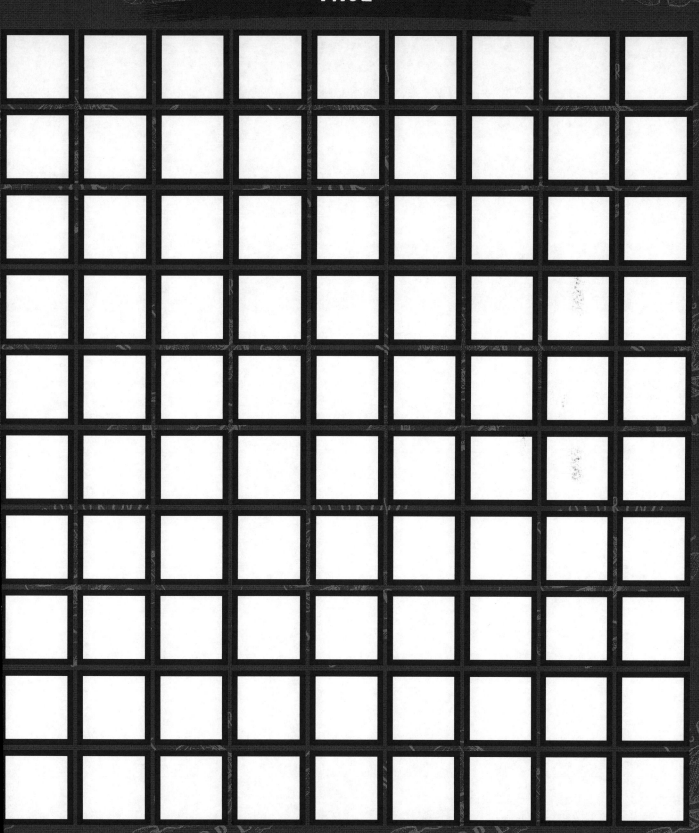

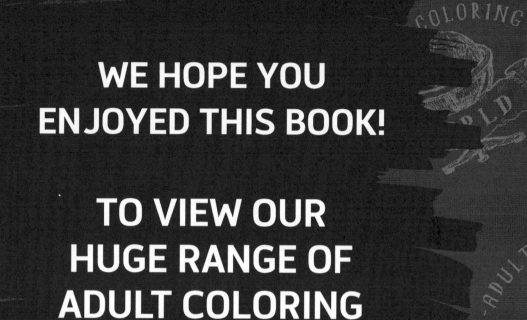

WE HOPE YOU
ENJOYED THIS BOOK!

TO VIEW OUR
HUGE RANGE OF
ADULT COLORING
BOOKS, VISIT
OUR WEBSITE
TODAY:

ADULTCOLORINGWORLD.NET

Made in the USA
Middletown, DE
19 January 2017